THE OLD AND THE NEW WORLD WE LIVE IN

How to survive
First thing in the morning
Praise the Lord
Lunchtime
Praise the Lord
Evening
Praise the Lord
Bedtime
Praise the Lord

God Bless you in your travels
If you want to survive
Do unto others as you would
Have others do unto you

Follow all of his instructions from the Bible. Goodbye to the old world and welcome to the new world. And a happy New Year, 2023! I'm just waiting to see what is to be.

ELIZABETH MOTO

ISBN 979-8-88943-469-6 (paperback)
ISBN 979-8-88943-470-2 (digital)

Christian Faith Publishing
832 Park Avenue
Meadville, PA 16335
www.christianfaithpublishing.com

Printed in the United States of America

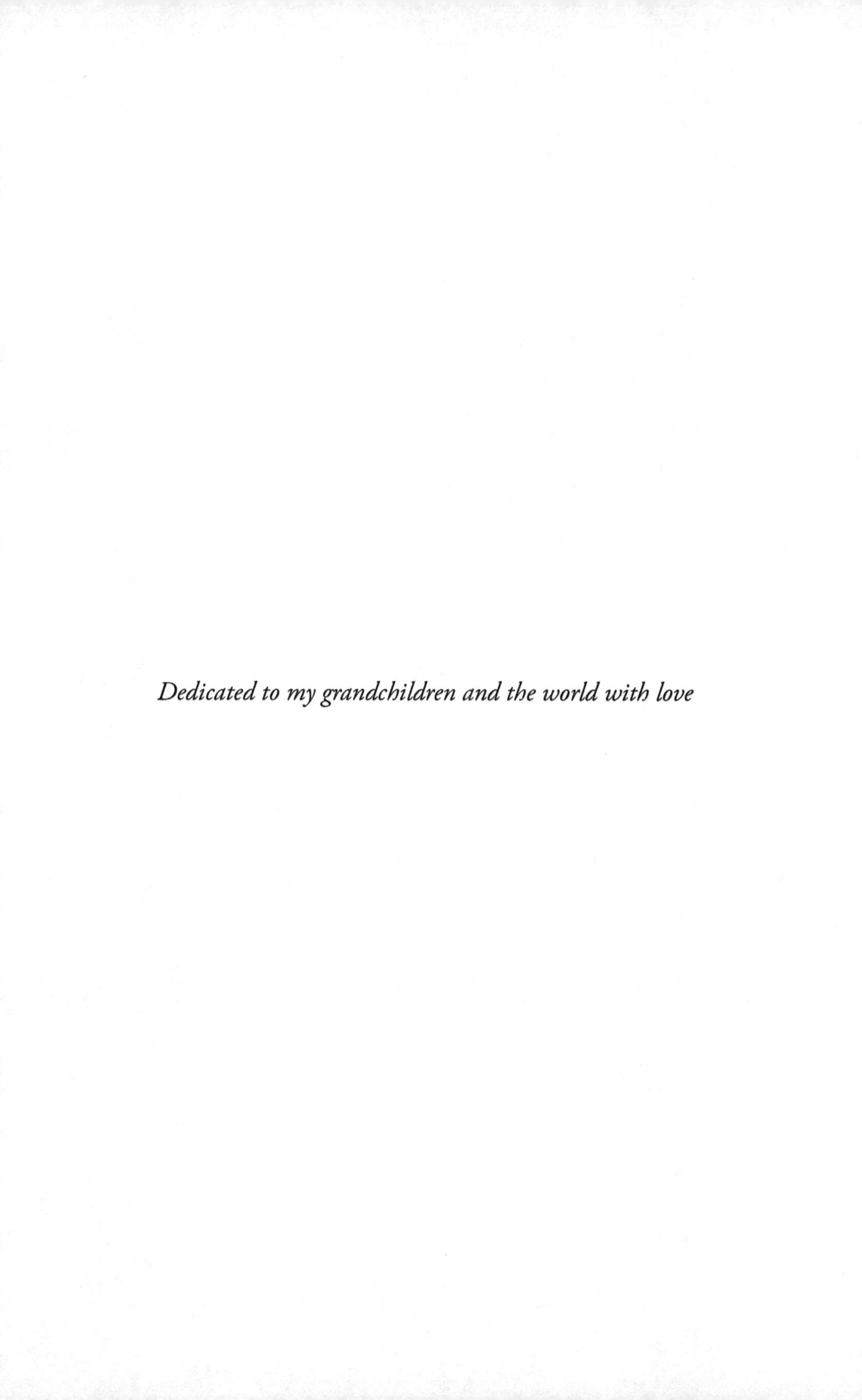

Dedicated to my grandchildren and the world with love

Our New World Needs Major Repairs

It's All Messed Up

The reason things are out of control today is that there are so many people that don't trust the system anymore. And the reason for this is the different techniques that have been used over and over again, yet nothing has changed. This is why people believe things never will.

We are living in a world of confusion with nowhere to go and no one to turn to. The system has taken control of everything that exists. Promises, promises, promises. It started in the Garden of Eden with Adam and Eve's disobedience to God and the manipulator, the snake, who has been slipping in and out of our lives for centuries, trying everyone.

The system needs a thorough cleaning, and it starts with the White House and voting. We are limited to two teams: Democrat or Republican. You're either one or the other. Another thing is that we should get to know these people we are voting for. We hear their names here and there before voting, and that's about it. After that, we have a short period of time before the vote, then we have a short amount of time to decide who we should vote for. Some people take the easiest way out and vote straight Democrat or straight Republican because they are in a hurry and in the middle, people in front of you and people behind you.

My suggestion? Not that it will mean anything, but I suggest the people that are getting paid to work in the polls go to work not only when it's time to vote but before. Find out what the people think.

Testimony of My New Book

When I started writing this book about one year after my first book, *Trapped in the Middle Thinking No Way Out*, I was so proud of myself. I was proud because it was done so much faster than the first one. All of a sudden, it came to a halt. I couldn't go any further, and I wondered why. The spirit said to me that the Bible says in Proverbs 27:1, "Boast not thy self of tomorrow for thou knowth not what a day may bring forth," and I recognized I felt really proud.

Then another thought came to me. I remembered that when things don't go your way, that means God is rearranging them, and that he did. *The back of my first book* said that if he—meaning God— is not pleased with what you are doing, he will shut the door. And along came COVID-19. The front of my first book said *Trapped*, and that is where we are today. When I wrote that book, I asked Author House to make it worldwide, knowing nothing about COVID-19 at all.

He didn't just shut the door on me with my second book. He also shut the whole world down, which tells me he is not pleased with what's going on in this world. We need to rearrange and pray it's not too late, and if it is, you better get ready really quickly because everything is done in God's time. And we have no idea when that is. No one knows the day or the hour.

Our Next Issue

We have no say in the way our kids are raised because the system has control. They teach our children all the things they are doing today from birth and until the time they leave this earth.

They are taught to be adults as soon as they can utter their first word. They don't know what it is like to have a child's life anymore, and we are not allowed to interfere. The system teaches them through phones, laptops, and TV shows how to be violent, curse, smoke, and drink alcohol; and don't forget sex, guns, and drugs. Once they learn all these things, then they are put in a situation they have no control over.

The system has the nerve to say, "We wonder why these kids act like they do." Now you don't have to wonder anymore, you know. Even some of our songwriters knew what was coming and tried to warn us through songs like "What's Going On" by Marvin Gaye, "A Ball of Confusion" by the Temptations, "Respect" by Aretha Franklin, and "A Whole New World" by Peabo Bryson, which we are living in today.

So many obstacles have been put in our paths, but let's look beyond the past and forward to the future, pray about it, and go to work so that we can have a better tomorrow. We were left with too many testimonies to give up now. When you think about giving up, think about Rosa Parks and the underground railroad as well as Martin Luther King Jr.'s "I Have a Dream," and don't forget "Put them Bibles back in school."

Tough Times

(I started writing this book in 2017, and now it is 2021)

Here are a few things to help us make it through these tough times were are going through:

1. Get to know God through prayer and supplication.
2. Pray without ceasing, thanking God for all he has done for you and all he is going to do for you.
3. Stop throwing your money away. Give it to the glory of God. He doesn't ask for much. Believe and receive.
4. If you have a dollar, give ten cents. Don't worry what other people think. This is between you and the Lord.
5. Stop thinking like the world. Use what God gave you: common sense. It's free. Not too many things are free.
6. Be patient. God does things in his own time. He told us in the *Word* that he may not be there when we want him to be but that he's always right on time.
7. Don't ever think that you can use God. He will end up using you. Remember, he is three in one: God the Father, the Son, and the *Holy* Spirit. Start reading.
8. Follow and obey all the commandments and instructions from the Bible.
9. After you have learned to communicate with the Lord, make sure you are prepared to take instructions.

Have a pen and paper in each room of your home so when he speaks, you can write it down the way he gave it to you, not the way you think it should be.

Psalm 150:6

God Sharing

Bible References Relating to the Use of Herbs

God Almighty has given us herbs to cure and cleanse our bodies. Let us not ignore what God has given us. The Bible speaks often of herbs and their benefit to mankind. This is a brief study of what God has said in his Word, *the Bible*:

> And God said, Behold, I have given you every herb, bearing seed, which is upon the face of all the earth, and every tree, in which is the fruit of a tree yielding seed; to you it shall be for meat. And to every beast of the earth, and to every fowl of the air, and to everything that creepeth, upon the earth, wherein there is life, I have given every green herb for meat: and it was so. (Genesis 1:29–30)

One of the first things Moses instructed the Israelites to do was clean their household things, then wash both their clothes and their bodies. Next, he instructed them to change their lustful diet of the flesh, which they freely indulged in, in Egypt. He knew their diet had to change if they were to survive. He began teaching them to live on simple nourishing food and use herbs for their medicine. He taught the Israelites that the grass and herbs of the fields were for the cattle and man's consumption (Psalm 104:14, Leviticus 11).

The prophet Ezekiel foresaw the diet during the millennial reign. He declared that the fruit of the trees would be for man's meat and that the leaves on the trees would serve as man's medicine (Ezekiel 47:12).

King Solomon was the wisest man that ever lived. He coupled herbs along with love (Proverbs 15:17).

Paul reminds us that if we continue to pollute or defile our temple, God will allow it to be destroyed. Your body is the temple of God. You must keep it holy and clean by not performing ungodly deeds and by not defiling it with poisonous food—food that gives you nothing in the way of nourishment (1 Corinthians 3:17).

Daniel said he would not defile himself with a portion of the king's meat, nor with wine. On the example of Daniel, we should not weaken and defile our body just because we find ourselves in the company of people that lust after their belly. Consider the penalty for those that make a god out of their belly (Philippian 3:19).

If we as God's children and his creation would only go back to God's original design for the family. Where sickness would be rare instead of common, we could truly know the joy of the abundant life that God planned for us on the planet Earth.

The Scripture teaches us that God's blessing to man has been his gift of herbs for our nourishment and healing. If we are wise, we will thank God Almighty and use his gift wisely. *What is your choice?*

Herbally yours,
Elizabeth Moto

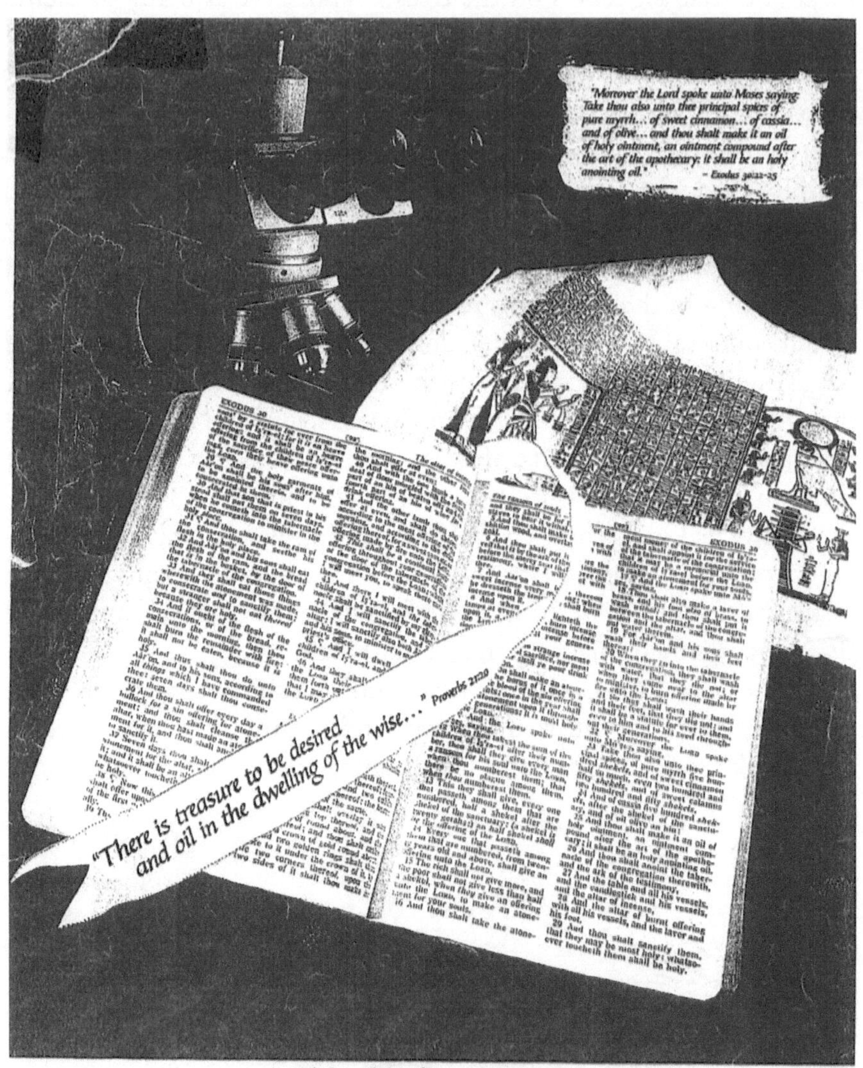

"Moreover the Lord spoke unto Moses saying:
Take thou also unto thee principal spices of
pure myrrh... of sweet cinnamon... of cassia...
and of olive... and thou shalt make it an oil
of holy ointment, an ointment compound after
the art of the apothecary: it shall be an holy
anointing oil."
- Exodus 30:22-25

"There is treasure to be desired
and oil in the dwelling of the wise..." Proverbs 21:20

The Bible

Oils

This is another product that has been around since the beginning of time. Read Exodus 30:20–25. It explains about the holy ointment. We can use oils in a variety of ways. Some of the oils are listed below, and they can also be diffused.

1. *Angelica.* Angelica has been referred to as the oil of the angels.
2. *Bergamot.* Uplifting.
3. *Clove.* Old-time remedy for tooth pain.
4. *Lavender.* Calms the atmosphere.
5. *Peppermint.* Opens your airways and makes it easier to breathe. It also calms the stomach with just a sniff. Do not use if you have acid reflux.
6. *Rosemary.* Your best infection fighter and also good for allergy sufferers. This is also good hair-growth stimulation and blood circulation.
7. *Valor.* Good for itching.
8. *Menthol.* Similar uses as no. 5, peppermint. It's good for clearing the chest of congestion.

PS: Make sure you check with your doctor first with the use of oil and all other products. Also check out herbal teas they have for a great night's sleep and healing.

Here are some oxygen-supplying plants:

1. Any rubber plant (Gebera, aloe, etc.)
2. Peace lily (also an air purifier)
3. Peperomia (also an air purifier)
4. Weeping fig

Raindrop
TECHNIQUE®
V-6
Ortho Ease
YOUNG LIVING
ESSENTIAL OILS

GOD SHARED (WHY CAN'T WE? I LOVE SHARING)

1. *Garlic.* Garlic is great for keeping your blood pressure under control and great on baked white potatoes with parsley and a little butter or margarine, whichever you prefer. Then you won't need salt. Salt is a killer.
2. *Parsley.* Parsley is known to keep your kidneys operating properly. It also relieves water retention and bloating. Sprinkle on noodles. And it can be used in salads.
3. *Dill.* Dill is helpful in relieving gas and heartburn.
4. *Ginger.* Using ginger is a good way to bring out the flavors in meat and other foods. Use ginger, and you will only need a pinch of salt.
5. *Italian seasoning.* It's very good because it has multiple herbs in it. It's great seasoning for stews, soups, and more with multicolored peppers and onions.
6. *Cayenne and chili peppers.* They are good sources of painkillers and put a great flavor in greens. I have been using them for years. Also try jalapeños.
7. *Turmeric.* Turmeric is said to be good for rheumatoid arthritis and carpal tunnel syndrome. It has vitamins A, C, and E in it.
8. *Oregano.* This herb has many chemicals that help control cough.
9. *Chamomile.* This is good for indigestion and sleep support.
10. *Mint.* This herb opens up your airways.

Make sure you check with your doctor first, and always start herbs slow to see how they affect your body. We also have healing teas.

My Sharing

Churches and Scriptures

Over the years, I have been a member of several churches, trying to find one where I could really help people. After my beloved husband passed away, I returned to my hometown of Philadelphia, Pennsylvania. I joined the Church of the Redeemer. I was there for several years until the Lord inspired me to write *Trapped in the Middle Thinking No Way Out*. Shortly after that, I had found the church of my dreams one block from where I lived. But COVID-19 stepped in, and I started watching church on_Zoom. Now I watch churches on TV, so I decided to help other organizations who go out and help those people we know who need help. It has been a blessing to me, and I feel good about it.

My belief is that instead of having so many small churches on every corner, they should join forces together and become several large churches. After all, the Lord did say that when we learn his Word, we should go out and spread it across the land. The 10 percent that we give to the church is for the upkeep of the church, and it keeps the doors open for the unsaved. Then the church would have extra money to purchase a van for the unfortunate and seniors who have no transportation but would love to be there. *Take action.*

All material shared, I saved over the years.

Scriptures

The Lord is my Shepherd. (Psalm 23:1)

Blessed is the man that walketh not in the counsel of the ungodly. (Psalm 1:1)

Our Father [and more do some research]. (Matthew 6:9)

Finally, be strong in the Lord and in the strength of his might. (Ephesians 6:10)

The LORD himself goes before you and will be with you; he will never leave you nor forsake you. Do not be afraid; do not be discouraged. (Deuteronomy 31:8)

The LORD will keep you from all harm he will watch over your life. [And if you are harmed, he will be there to take you out of your pain; he will not let you suffer if there is no cure. All things work together for good.] (Psalm 121:7)

And we know that God causes everything to work together for the good of those who love God and are called according to his purpose for them. For God knew his people in advance, and he chose them to become like his Son, so that his

Son would be the firstborn among many brothers and sisters. (Romans 8:28–29)

And my God will supply all your needs according to the riches of his glory in Christ Jesus. (Philippians 4:19)

[God is our refuge.] You are my hiding place; you will protect me from trouble and surround me with songs of deliverance. (Psalm 32:7)

The Lord is a refuge for the oppressed, a stronghold in times of trouble. (Psalm 9:9)

The Lord is good, a stronghold in the day of trouble; he knows those who take refuge in him. (Nahum 1:7)

[He comforts.] Blessed are they that mourn: for they shall be comforted. (Matthew 5:4)

He comforts us whenever we suffer. That is why whenever other people suffer, we are able to comfort them by using the same comfort we have received from God. (2 Corinthians 1:4)

Give all your worries and cares to God, for he cares about you. (1 Peter 5:7)

And call upon me in the day of trouble; I will deliver you, and you shall glorify me. (Psalm 50:15)

Keep your Bible open twenty-four hours a day to Psalm 91. Regarding your protection, remember that there is no higher power than God (Romans 13:1).

Higher Powers Ephesians 6:10–18

Always continue to research. Whatever we humans say, we should research in the Bible to back it up, including me.

Important scriptures

1. Matthew 24 (signs of the time)
2. Matthew 7 (Judge not; pray about it.)
3. Matthew 6:9 (how to pray)
4. Mark 13:6 ("Many shall come in my name saying I am Christ and deceive you." [Be aware.])
5. First Peter 4:13 was left out.
6. James 11-8 (Do not waver.)

Important info

1. Ephesians 6:10–18 (Put on the whole armor of God.)
2. A pastor is a shepherd, a clergyman, or a priest in charge of a church.
3. A minister is a Christian preacher or person acting for another, carrying out his orders of a clergyman or a priest.
4. A bishop is supposed to be blameless and a husband of one wife (1 Timothy 3:1–5).
5. I couldn't find anything on a pope listed in the Bible (help).

Your Body

God gave you a good body. Show him that you appreciate it by giving it the best you have to offer. Take care of it. Your body is like a temple. When you build it, you have to provide it with a good foundation. If not, it will fall apart.

Don't use anything that is damaging to it. Sometimes the more it cost, the more damaging it is. Think about it and then think about the amount of money you could have been saving. Never put medicine in your system before putting something in your stomach unless it specifies that it must be taken before eating. Use plenty of fruits and vegetables. They are the source of good health in season. Out of season, use them frozen. Make sure you read all the ingredients and nutrition facts.

Salt and sugar—they are the killers. Salt leads to high blood pressure, and sugar and starch lead to diabetes. Do everything in moderation. That's what the Bible says. Some food you do not like the taste of, but your body still needs them for their nutritional value, so you need to find something to substitute for them.

I found a good company called Puritan's Pride. They have very good products and deals, but again, you must check with your doctor first. I have been taking their products for years with no complaints. Remember, each person's system is different. Now, today you have blenders, so you can blend all of the food you don't like. So now you have a choice—no excuses.

Marriage and Family

If you are thinking of marriage, think twice. Remember, this is supposed to be for life, according to the Bible. So I believe you should do some research first. Why? Because the best in a person always comes out early. So you should meet the immediate family first to give you some idea of what you will be dealing with concerning your future and also your future generation. Remember, the best in a person always comes out first. Also, remember that every child needs a father and a mother. Now, if you don't want that responsibility, there are other options.

Parents

We as parents teach our children through the way we conduct ourselves. They are constantly listening and watching us. This is how they learn. This is also why sometimes we hear people say, "He is just like his father" or "She is just like her mother." This tells us people are constantly watching you, even your kids.

Just for laughs

Kids don't realize that parents work really hard to provide for them. They seem to think money grows on trees. They want what they want, and if they can't have it, they will put on a good show. One lady told me she bought her granddaughter a nice pair of sneakers. She gave them to her granddaughter. Her reply was "I only wear Nikes."

Her grandmother said, "Okay, give them back to me." Grandmother took them home and wrote *Nikes* on them and gave them back to her, saying, "Here are your Nikes."

I had a good laugh. It made my day.

GERMS

One of the worst things you can do is share germs. We have so many people who do just that every day. When my children were growing up, I made them aware of this at an early age. I made sure that each one had their own plate, glass, and cup. It made each one feel special because they were able to pick their own color and design. They were also taught that you never leave anything in your glass unattended because anything can take place in your absence. Never put your hands in a bag that has been previously opened; the person who put their hand in that bag before you might've just gone to the bathroom and forgot to wash their hands or had just sneezed. We never know. So it's better to have individual bags. Also, these days, we should only give hugs with your faces in opposite directions. No kisses, not even your children; they could give you a cold or the flu. In this new age, the flu is dangerous. Do not teach your children to kiss you in the mouth because they will think that is okay to do with others, especially with strangers. Don't forget about COVID-19, the new dangerous flu, and more. Like, what's next?

Words Can Destroy You

Be careful how you use them because they can make or break you or someone else. Think before you use them, or you may end up paying for them sooner or later. Remember, some people take things differently from others. It's all according to their situation at the time. Don't take chances.

Another thing is to learn all you can today. Don't depend on your cell phone having all the answers because if you did, then what? And also, all our transactions are being done on the computer and phones, and the writing is so small and lengthy. You don't have time to read all of it because the system says to keep moving, and God tells us to be still. What is your choice? Common sense, or keep moving?

Give the Lord a little time because this is where all your instructions and knowledge come from. So don't be so lazy that you can't give him some of your time. You will be blessed because it will open your eyes.

These words came from a plaque that I have, so
I thought about sharing them with you.

Give and Take

Give yourself time to think
For it is the force of power
Take time to pray
For it is the secret of everlasting youth
Give yourself time to read
For it is the foundation of wisdom
Take time to pray
For it is the greatest power on earth
Take time to love and be loved
For it is a God-given privilege
Take time to be friendly
For it is the path to happiness
Give yourself time to laugh
For it is the sound of the soul
Take time to give yourself to someone else
For time is too short to be selfish
Give and take
For this is the key to…
Success, heaven, and happiness
(Author unknown, but this poem is too
beautiful for it to go to waste.)

This idea came to me during the Christmas of 2016. It's called sharing with others. I had so many things that I wasn't using. I needed to get rid of them. The spirit said to me, "Why not share? Someone else may need them or can use them."

I lived in an apartment complex, and that was perfect, so I wrote a note. It read, "If you need it, take it. If not, let someone else get it, or give it to someone else who can use it. It's called sharing. If you sow, you will reap. I've been sharing all my life, but now I decided to expand. Enclosed, you may find some important material you might be able to use if not now, then maybe in your future, about which we are all wondering, *What's next?*"

By the way, all the items I put out were gone in one day. Praise God! He put me in business. Give and take. Let's start the year off right!

Keep your system cleansed so you won't be burdened with infections because that's the killer.

Spray shoe soles with a disinfectant spray or clean them with wipes. Watch where you walk when outside. Someone could have spit on the ground, and you might come along and step in it.

Have a shoe rack at the entrance of your door so the shoes can be cleaned now or later. Wash your hands frequently.

If you can, get an air purifier for your home or apartment to keep dirty air out, and get a humidifier to put moisture in the air. If your home is dry or if you have allergies, these are helpful. Make sure you check with your doctor for us about all of these.

Put oxygen-supplying plants around your home, especially if you have allergies. Keep an emergency kit in your home at all times and also a Life Alert necklace. I'm looking for a watch from Life Alert because I don't like a cord around my neck, and because of my allergies, I may itch.

Just a reminder: Be on the watch; the snake is in the garden, busy doing what he promised. We as Christians should be spreading the Word and giving testimonies. Please share.

Spiritual

If you would like to write a book, *know* that writing a book is neither easy or hard if you go about it the right way. But you must follow instructions.

1. Consult your Lord and Savior Jesus Christ through prayer and ask for guidance.
2. Be prepared to take instructions.
3. Place a pencil and a pad in each room of your home so that when you get instructions from the Lord, you can write them down exactly the way he gave it to you because later, you might have it all mixed up, and this will cause delay.
4. Always write with a pencil just in case you make a mistake and have to correct it; you'll be able to go back and erase it. If you write it with a pen, you won't be able to erase it, and you'll end up spending extra money. Mistakes are usually hidden, and you won't know until you go back and read it again. I found out the hard way after writing my first book. I didn't realize how many mistakes I had made until I went back and read it. I actually saw them and had to pay for them, and that hurt my pocketbook. But I learned a lesson, and I can pass it on to you.

SHARING

The man WHISPERED, "God, speak to me."
And a meadowlark sang.
But the man did not HEAR.

So the man YELLED, "God, speak to me!"
And thunder rolled across the sky.
But the man did not LISTEN.

The man LOOKED around and said,
"God, let me see you."
And a star shined brightly, but the man did not SEE.

And the man SHOUTED, "God, show me a miracle!"
And a new baby was born.
But the man did not NOTICE.

So the man cried out in despair,
"TOUCH me, God, and let me know you are here!"
Whereupon God reached down and touched the man,
But—the man BRUSHED the butterfly away and
WALKED on.

[Don't walk on. *Listen.*]
(Author unknown)

THE CHRISTIAN GARDEN

5 Rows of Peas

1. Prayer
2. Preparedness
3. Politeness
4. Promptness
5. Perseverance

3 Rows of Squash

1. Squash Gossip
2. Squash Criticism
3. Squash Indifference

5 Rows of Lettuce

1. Let us love one another
2. Let us be unselfish
3. Let us be trustful
4. Let us be faithful
5. Let us be loyal

(author unknown)

ALLERGIES

I started researching for other alternatives when I found out I was allergic to so many different things including medicines and didn't know what to do. Even the doctor told me, "You are allergic to so many things. We don't know what to give you anymore," so I researched. Most of the products I use are made in the USA, fragrance-free, and dermatologist tested; otherwise, I will break out and itch like crazy.

That's when I discovered aloe and HealthWorks Omega-3—a special fish oil. Please remember that regarding anything I share, make sure you check with your health-care provider or your doctor.

Aloe

I have been using aloe products since 1982, and I still do. I started out with a company called Aloe Charm. The president of the company was Rivka Seltzer. She was bought out by a company called Herbalife. Today I can give aloe a roaring applause for its uses. I was allergic to so many products, but aloe worked wonders for me.

Now, today you can buy the leaves of the aloe plant in grocery stores, near the vegetables. You can also buy the gel of the plant in the drugstore, near your lotions. It is one of the best products for burns, cuts, and abrasions but not major burns. Aloe also soothes arthritis. Be sure to consult with your doctor.

The aloe plant can be grown at home. They are also sold in stores like Home Depot, Lowe's, and Walmart. Growing instructions can be found in the next page.

V with your doctor.

Aloe Plant Care Instructions

Light
- Place in a room where there is bright light.
- Will tolerate full sun.

Water
- In spring and summer, allow the soil to dry between waterings.
- In fall and winter, water sparingly; keep your aloe dry.

Temperature
- Ideal temperature is 19–25°C (65–77°F).

Feeding
- In spring and summer, fertillize monthly.
- Do not fertilize in the fall and winter.

Of Interest to You
- Aloe vera, also known as the Barbadoes aloe, is a succulent member of the lily family. Aloes are found in nearly all the warm or arid areas of the world. Since ancient times, man has known of the medicinal qualities of aloe vera. Among the earliest were the Greeks, who, in fourth-century BC, were using "bitter aloes" (aloe vera) in the treatment of different ills. The soothing qualities of its gel, when used on cuts and burns, has long made aloe a household necessity in South Africa, Java, the Philippines, Greece, Egypt, India, South America, and Japan. Today its popularity is spreading throughout America. Many households keep an aloe vera plant in the kitchen as an instant first aid for minor cuts and burns. The gel is contained inside the fleshy leaves. Simply cut off a half-inch from the long tip of the leaf and squeeze the gel from the center. GROWN IN CANADA.

ALOE VERA

The Medicine Plant

For Indoors Outdoors or Patio

THE MEDICINE PLANT

ALOE VERA

The Wonder Herb

The plant that is used for many medicinal purposes

Grows easily in your home, patio, or outdoors, where it will withstand cold down to 34 degrees. It prefers partial shade, rich soil with good drainage, and watering only when dry. Transplant it into a larger pot after about eight months from purchase of plant.

NON-WARRANTY

Nurserymen's Exchange, Inc. gives no warranty, express or implied, as to the description of fitness of its plants for any particular purpose or use, and recommends that you see a physician for any medical problems.

MY OLD WORLD

Sequel to *Trapped in the Middle Thinking No Way Out*

Based on a true story by Elizabeth Moto. Narrator of the book *Trapped in the Middle Thinking No Way Out* still guided by the Holy Spirit.

There is no doubt in my mind that God makes a way out of no way. Look what he did with two lost souls.

David Moto

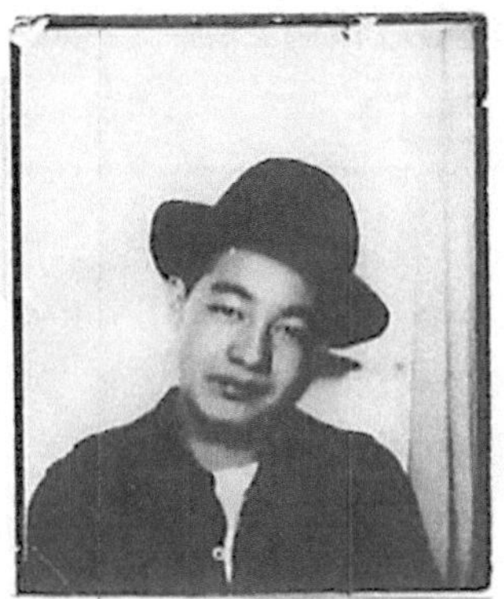

He didn't get to know his father.

Elizabeth White Bey

I didn't get to know my father.

Man has his way of tearing us apart, but God has his way of putting us back together. We were married fifty years until his parting from this world. The lesson I learned from this was that every child needs a father and a mother.

TESTIMONY FROM MY OLD WORLD

God makes a way out of no way. When I wrote my first book, I had no idea what to put on the front cover except God the Father, the Son, and the Holy Spirit. But God stepped in again and put everything else right in place. The Holy Spirit said to me, "Why not put that picture you have of yourself that your husband handed to you on his deathbed? It holds a lot of memories for you. That is the only picture you have of yourself as a youngster, and this is the first book you ever wrote. Your husband saved it all the years you were together, and you didn't even know he had it until his passing."

<<Original below>>
Restored photo on the front cover of *Trapped in The Middle Thinking No Way Out*

Young Elizabeth

III

SOME THINGS I REMEMBER FROM MY OLD WORLD

I was too young to remember all things, but here are a few. I sometimes wonder and travel back down memory lane around the corner from where I live now to where I was birthed.

I was told my grandmother was a midwife and that she birthed me in the month of May, in the year of 1937, at our home on 2515 Morton Street, Philadelphia, Pennsylvania, near the overhead bridge on Twenty-Fifth Street. I called her Grandmom, but I was told her name was Georgianna Mary Mellissa McBride Stevens, and her husband's name was Benjamin Stevens.

I have a picture of them in my first book, *Trapped in The Middle Thinking No Way Out.* The next thing I remember was that we moved to 1538 Naudain Street in Philadelphia, Pennsylvania. After that, we moved to Williamstown, New Jersey, on 134 E. Malaga Road. At the age of sixteen, I decided to leave home with the direction of the Holy Spirit. I left and returned to Philadelphia to live with my school teacher Sister Olive M. Bey at 2623 Manton Street, one block from where I was born. I had her permission earlier.

Everyone that was Moorish American. Their last name was either El or Bey. My father's name was Samuel White Bey, so my name was Elizabeth White Bey. When I married David L. Moto, I dropped White and Bey, reason being I never had any association with my father. I dropped Bey because I became a Christian and to do unto others as I would have others do unto me.

IV

ANOTHER TESTIMONY

When I wrote my previous book, I said this would never happen again, that I would never write another one. But I found out later that you don't say no to the Holy Spirit because he will turn you completely around. My new book is proof of the power of the Holy Spirit. How to survive in the new world we live in? And with the things that are going on today, if you care, how can you say no?

Our First Mistake

Taking the Bible out of schools was one of the worst things the system could have done because that was our guide to live a healthy, happy, and prosperous life.

We don't have common sense anymore because we don't have choices that make you think. That tells me that your choices are made by someone else. Everything in the Bible makes you think. Society today doesn't give you time to think. So you just follow the rules that man has made for you. You don't like following rules, so you make your own and do what you want to do because you don't have time to think that you are confused. And that leads to confusion. That tells me we need to go back to the basics, which is the Bible.

SLAVERY

Some people believe that slavery is over. I say it still exists today. It's just done in a more sophisticated manner. The difference is that it includes everyone—rich, middle-class, poor, Black, White, and the in-between.

1. *Credit cards.* Buy all you want and pay later. But don't be late, or late charges will be added. Please don't say were having a big sale. You're hooked.
2. *Phones.* Yes, we definitely need one in this society today, but guess what we become—more and more dependent on them. We can't remember anything anymore. A lot of people can't spell, write, or count. Why? Because we don't have to. Just ask Google or Siri. They will tell you the answer because you're busy, running, in a hurry all the time, and your brain is being deleted. So you say to yourself, "Well, let me grab a cigarette and calm down. I'll be okay."
3. *Smoking.* Look at what it costs and what damage it do to your health and well-being. Marijuana is said to help some illnesses, but look at what it can do to you—addiction. Now who do you turn to? Just think about that.
4. *Habits.* They are just like slavery; you get use to doing the same thing over and over again.

Let's go back to your phone. When we end a conversation, we normally say, "Bye," but there are other options like "I love you," "Peace," "God bless," "Talk to you later," and "Have a blessed day"; but we are always rushing and in a hurry to get... where? Think about this. Where does rushing get you? It's just another form of slavery; you are being put in a position where you have no choices or no one to turn to. Think about this. Get protection and put God in your life. There will always be worries, but you will have what you need to make it through. You just have to believe.

ANOTHER THOUGHT

Old people are sometimes referred to as old fogies or old bags, but guess what? They feel good because they have common sense and lot of knowledge. Try listening to them sometimes. Try using some of their techniques sometimes, and you'll find out they are not as feeble as you think they are. They're just using their brains, making it simple, also using their head. You better get all the info you can because we won't always be around. One day, we will be gone, and you will have to depend on your generation. If you can't make your own choices, that's slavery.

Something Extra

God created heaven and earth, which is the sky above us and the land below us. There are rivers, streams, trees, and all the greenery around us. What a beautiful view. Read the first book of the Bible. And I pray it will keep you interested long enough to continue reading and seeking more knowledge. Also read 1 Timothy 6:6–7 (money).

Satan

Stay on guard for Satan because he is on the loose. He warned us in the beginning that he would be there till the end. He's trying to get God's people confused, but if you are truly one of God's children, he can't confuse you because you're already prepared for it. We know our God is a god of peace. Satan is all about confusion. Be on the watch. When you see confusion, be silent, step aside, and move on.

Pastor Lovett at Tasker St. Missionary Baptist Church warned us on Sunday (August 28, 2022). His message was "Mind your own business." He just named it Pastor mind your own business "beautiful message." We would have a much better world to live in if we just mind our own business and move on.

Prayers

When praying to God, always remember to make sure you go to him through his Son, Jesus Christ, because no one can go to the Father except through his son.

Keep in mind, try to stay out of the hospital. Keep your house clean, both where you live and the one you live in, which is your temple. Give it a thorough cleaning every now and then because this is where your problems start. Then infections and diseases take over.

Shellfish triggers more infections than any other food we eat. Do some research and read Leviticus 11 in the Old Testament. In the New Testament, read Romans 14.

Cell phones are one of the most controlling tools we have. Whatever you do, don't let it control you. Your mind is a terrible thing to waste. If you lose that, you will have lost it all. Use it before you lose it.

I know your plate is full, but I have some dessert I couldn't hold back from. In the beginning, there was Satan. In the middle, there was Satan, and he told us he would be there in the end. Do not let him use you. Instead, use him. Keep him busy going around in circles, where there's no end, until he meets Jesus Christ and God. Hallelujah!

Robots

Right Now We Are Like Robots

We wait for someone to push our button to find out what and where our next move will be. But make sure it comes from the right source so that you are on the right track, the one with no detours, not the one that says, "Dead End Rd."

Let's be more like the devil but in a godly way. He's cunning. If he finds out you will not bend to his level, he leaves you alone for a while, go to the closest one to you, then come back later to see how you are doing. He never leaves you until God wins.

We can't give up either. We must be strong and keep on trying—no arguments.

I always say that when things don't go your way, remember that God is rearranging them for your benefit. Don't get upset. He knows what he's doing. Remember, God is omnipotent. He is also three in one. You can't beat him, so you might as well join him. Remember, this book was rearranged. This page was supposed to be up in the front, and now it is in the back. I was rushing, and God had to slow me down. So where did rushing get me? Back to where I started—a new beginning.

Remember, Satan is on the loose. Get him with the Word of God—no arguments.

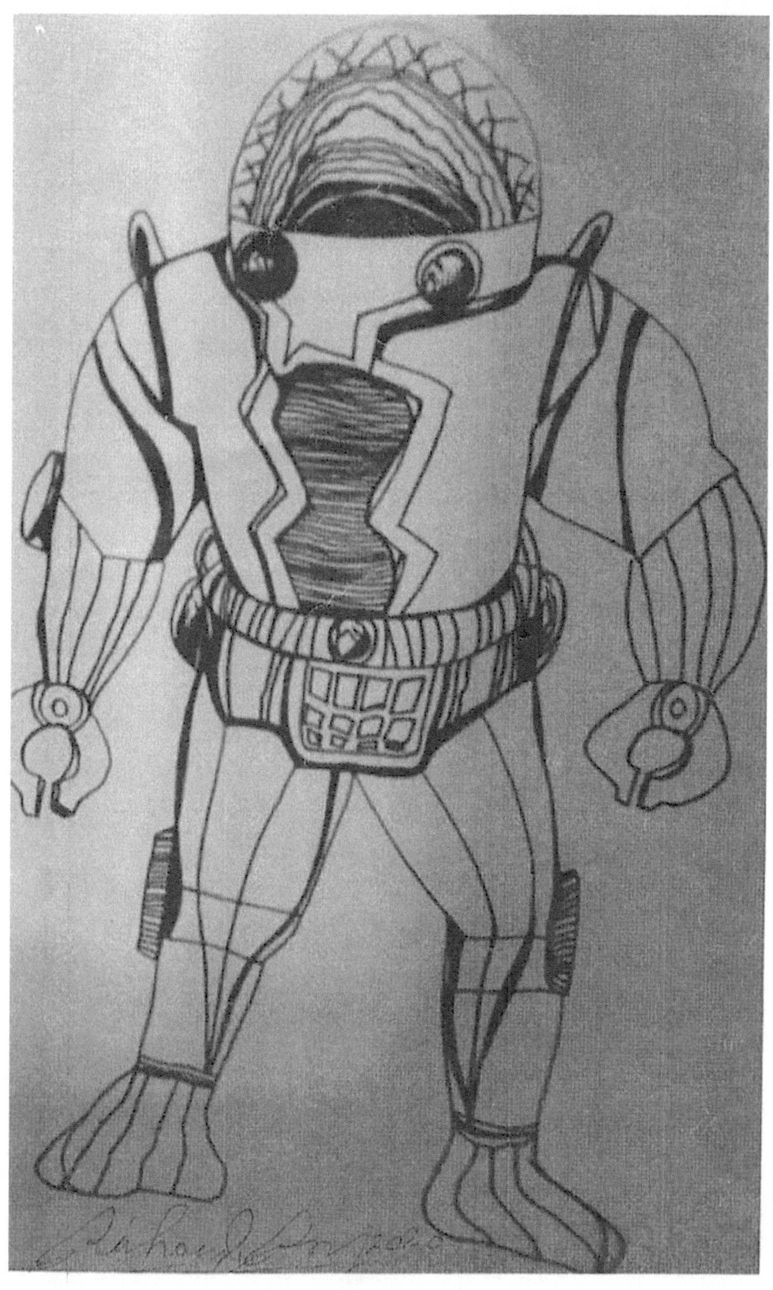

More Testimonies Since My Last Book

In the month of September, we had the big storms Harvey, Irma, and Jose in Florida. We were told it was the worst ever. The news said it would go down in history. My daughter Carmen and her family were stranded down in Florida. I prayed and prayed, and the good Lord stepped in to let me know I had nothing to worry about. He had everything under control. He spoke to me and said, "Think back, my child. Your husband's grandmother's name was Harvey. She is now deceased, and she's helping the Master watch over them. Also, remember that you gave your life to Christ. You're worry-free."

I could go on and on, but I've been instructed to finish this book so that it can help someone else.

PS: He will give you the desires of your heart and more, something you didn't even ask for. But you must ask and believe. Just be careful what you ask for.

TESTIMONY

My youngest son, Vincent, had a godmother named Ms. Thymes. We had been looking for her for about thirty years. Our church was having a trip going to the African American museum in Washington, DC. At the last moment, I decided to inquire about it and found out they had one ticket left, so I purchased it. Thank God I did because this was where I met the Thymes family again. My seat was directly across from them. I didn't know them, and they didn't know me because of the lapse of time. They were all grown up now and had families of their own.

Eventually, one of them said to me, "What is your first name?" and I told her, "Elizabeth." Then she said to me, "Oh my god, you used to sew for my mother," so I said to her, "What is your mother's name?

She replied, "Mrs. Thymes."

I asked her, "How is she?"

The reply was that she passed away in 2010, which was the same year my husband passed away. But we were living in North Carolina at that time, and they had also moved. That's how we lost contact with the family.

The Lord said he will supply all our needs (Philippians 4:19), and he did just that. But we are still waiting on a compensation bill to be passed. These victims have lost so many years of their lives. At least that might give them some of their dreams back, if they were compensated.

My son Vincent Moto has made some progress since the movie "after innocence" directed by Jessica Sanders. He received a citation from the commonwealth of Pennsylvania for being the first exoneree through the DNA he is now fighting for a compensation to be passed in Philadelphia. These victims have lost so many years of their lives. At least it might give them some of their dreams back if compensated.

Commonwealth of Pennsylvania

The House of Representatives
Citation

Whereas, this citation honors Vincent Moto as Pennsylvania's Historical Exoneree, for being the first to be exonerated through the advent of DNA evidence in criminal cases in 1996; and

Whereas, since Vincent's exoneration, he has endlessly and relentlessly fought for the expungement of his record; and

Whereas, after 25 years, Vincent's record was successfully expunged on February 17, 2021. He is fighting for a wrongfully convicted compensation bill to be passed in Pennsylvania; and

Whereas, as of July 23, 2021, Vincent will have been out of prison for 25 years; and

Whereas, Vincent is a member of and volunteers for RIGHT The Wrong Coalition and a few other advocacy groups for wrongfully convicted persons; and

Whereas, Vincent currently co-hosts MIC TEST Entertainment and provides a platform for up-and-coming local artists and talent to share their gifts with not only this city but the world; and

Whereas, Vincent is an awesome multi-talented musician, song-writer, composer, arranger and studio engineer who has helped many area youth, teens and young adults by opening his home studio for them to record free of charge. Vincent has provided free drum, piano, and guitar lessons as well.

Now therefore be it resolved, that the Pennsylvania House of Representatives and the Honorable Regina G. Young recognize Vincent Moto for being the first wrongfully convicted person in Pennsylvania to be exonerated through use of DNA evidence, his activism in ensuring that other wrongfully convicted Pennsylvanians receive justice through comprehensive policy, and his continued contributions to elevating the talents local artists across Philadelphia.

And directs, that a copy of this citation, sponsored by the Honorable Regina G. Young of Pennsylvania's 185th Legislative District, be transmitted to Vincent Moto.

Regina G. Young
State Representative
Pennsylvania House of Representatives
185th Legislative District

TESTIMONIES OF WHAT THE LORD CAN DO

Since I wrote my last book, someone very dear to me has gone home to be with the Lord: my brother, son, and father, Rev. Ezekiel G. Bey.

He was my brother because my mother birthed him, my son because I had to raise him because of my mother's illness, and my father because the Lord took over his life and made sure he went to seminary school to become a minister. Then he used my brother to introduce me to Christ and baptize me.

My what a marvelous God we serve. He is the only one that I know that will not let you down. He is the sunshine of my life.

I used to shed tears of sorrow, but now I shed tears of joy.

Ezekiel

Isaiah, Ezekiel, and Pupit

O how I loved them.

POEM

LIFE'S UPS AND DOWNS

Life is a mystery of ups and downs
The ups pick you up for you to continue your journey
The downs seem to go round and round
But through it all, thank God you are
able to call on the one who is able to
solve all problems, great and small
It seems like it's the end, but it's just the
beginning, so keep the faith
He will pick you up to run the race, and you
will be able to feel his grace

January 12, 2022

Feeling sorry for yourself does not
make you feel better; it pulls you down
Get up

The power of the Lord is here. Read Psalm 46 in the King James Version. This should leave no doubt in your mind who's in charge.

So we have to do it for the children because I had no one to do it for me. Message from my son Vincent Moto

LOVE LOVE LOVE
Love
LOVE LOVE LOVE

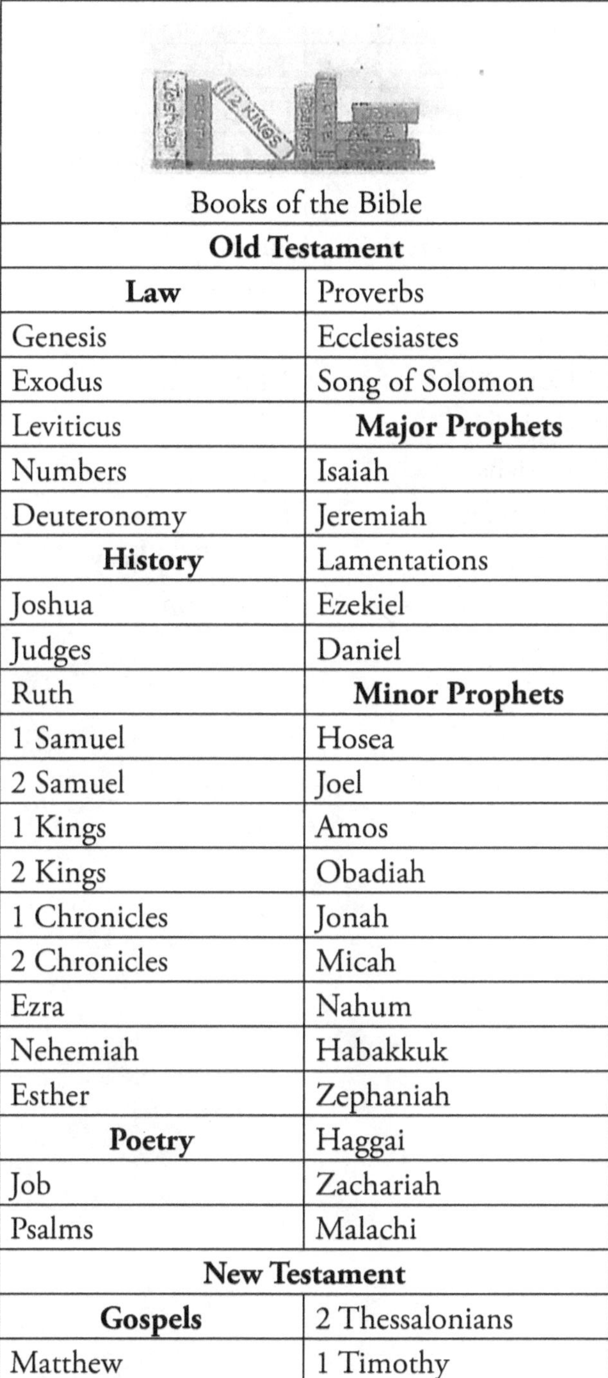

Books of the Bible

Old Testament	
Law	Proverbs
Genesis	Ecclesiastes
Exodus	Song of Solomon
Leviticus	**Major Prophets**
Numbers	Isaiah
Deuteronomy	Jeremiah
History	Lamentations
Joshua	Ezekiel
Judges	Daniel
Ruth	**Minor Prophets**
1 Samuel	Hosea
2 Samuel	Joel
1 Kings	Amos
2 Kings	Obadiah
1 Chronicles	Jonah
2 Chronicles	Micah
Ezra	Nahum
Nehemiah	Habakkuk
Esther	Zephaniah
Poetry	Haggai
Job	Zachariah
Psalms	Malachi
New Testament	
Gospels	2 Thessalonians
Matthew	1 Timothy

Mark	2 Timothy
Luke	Titus
John	Philemon
History	**General Letters**
Acts	Hebrews
Paul's Letters	James
Romans	1 Peter
1 Corinthians	2 Peter
2 Corinthians	1 John
Galatians	2 John
Ephesians	3 John
Philippians	Jude
Colossians	**Prophecy**
1 Thessalonians	Revelation

About the Author

With twelve years of schooling and no college degrees, Elizabeth asks you to look at what she turned out to be. She is a product of what God can do for the world to see. You can still learn all you can because in life, you will never know what you will need (she speaks from experience).